MW01230419

Hearts of the Winds

I Dedicate this Book

To the late
Tommie L. and Marjorie E. Williams

My parents who invited me into this life and gave me love, wisdom, truth of spirit and planted the seed of God's love within my heart through Jesus Christ.

This book is also dedicated to my children Torree, Brittany & Tramain
My grandchildren, my brothers, my sisters, nephews, nieces and every member of the Williams blood line that connects us.

To my many family members and friends who are too many to name, but in the words of my late grandmother who would say, "you know who you are"!

And to all,
Thank you for your love and understanding of me for who I am.

Above all,
Thank you Lord for your mercy, love, grace and kindness
To at last place the ink upon these pages of a dream I saw so long ago.

1 Corinthians 13:4-7 NIV Study Bible

Love is patient, love is kind.
It does not envy, it does not boast, it is not proud.
It is not rude, it is not self-seeking,
It is not easily angered, it keeps no record of wrongs.
Love does not delight in evil but rejoices with the truth.
It always protects, always trusts, always hopes, always preseveres.

My Introduction

Love ain't pain, love ain't fear,
Love ain't beating up on the one you clam to hold so dear.
And I mean mentally beating or physically beating someone.

Love is a feeling of joy, a feeling of happiness, a feeling of kindness and a feeling that you share with hopes of having that same love in return.

If you have any kind of love within you, this book should place a smile upon your face. We have all experienced love from one degree to another. Some have experienced love more than others, while some have only a limited amount of its joy and the pain which sometimes follows.

Yet no one, no matter how rich you are or how poor, how strong or weak, we all share one common feeling within. We all yearn for a feeling of love, that's because it's a natural thing.

Even some of the most hateful people crave love deep from within. If not, then why do they try so hard to be accepted by someone?

Love has many faces many writers will write, yet it has but one rule and that rule is to love, which follows patience, respect, forgiveness, understanding, communication, and kindness.

I claim not to be a Doctor Phil or a Steve Harvey with my message. But what I do offer is my own personal experience with love, in hopes that there may be some connection to enlighten your relationship.

I share with you memories from my heart, memories from the hearts of some I know and memories from the imagination. Please read these words from so many years that it took me to prepare this tasteful meal of this mental kitchen, as you feed your mind with one man's mental culinary delights.

Words of the heart
which flow
with no beginning
with no end
yet
they leave something
for the mind to ponder.

" Never fear love, for there is no fear in love, only fear in fear"

Table of Contents Chapter I

The Heart That Beats   *Chapter II*

The World in Which We Live   *Chapter III*

Memories   *Chapter IV*

My Love Is

The pages you are about to read are from the pages of my heart.
There are a few added hearts of friends in which I put myself in their place and
made them my own.

Chapter I

A day in life

Some day my tomorrow will be my today

Some day my today will be my yesterday

Some day my yesterday will only be a memory

Of my dreams to become my visions

My visions to become my reality

My prayers are the dreams that I take to God in silence
  with the faith of becoming real.

-t.alfonso williams

…… …… …… …..*we all carry dreams in our hearts and minds, whether they are, to better ourselves or others. To create or to improve our way of life, we are but humans that always have dreams.*

Art of Whisper

Soft and low
Sweet and slow
Words of love easy as they flow

Close upon the ear
Through the waterfalls of the mind
For only her to hear

Gently my words flow, down the river of conciseness'
She close her eyes
Moans and smile
To answer, yes I know

Soft and low
Sweet and slow
Words of love gently as I go

A kiss is placed upon her cheek
Soft and sweet
Without words to speak

Soft and low
Sweet and slow

Soft and low
Sweet and slow

So gentle
As I go

....do I need to explain, the art of whispering softly into her ear, the sensual words which makes her happy from ear to ear. For lovers only!!!

A Morsel

Other men have come
  and chipped away at your heart
    like thieves in the dark

For I have come
  to return in you
    all the love your heart
      once upon a time knew

Never to be judged
  as the rest, for I am here
    to take your mind, from any mental stress

Love me like the one
  which you hide secretly
    within your heart

Only to share
  just
    a small and simple morsel
      of your selfishness.

-t.alfonso williams

..........many times you have been hurt, so now you hide you, inside of you.

Lepidoptera

Setting in my garden
  the sun at my back
    my eyes catch her entrance

Beauty she unveils
  her long slender body
    her beautiful black silky gown with dazzling colors to astound
      yet she has never made not one sound

She dances from here to there
  she dance and she dances
    while displaying her beauty everywhere

Moving about without a care
  moving about her freedom is in the air

No time to care
  no time to care
    she continues to dance
      I continue to stare

From flower to flower she moves about
  from flower to flower without a care
    without a doubt

My garden she has made a place to room
  my garden is only one
    of her so many homes.

-t.alfonso williams

… … … …..she is only a butterfly, now what did you think that I was talking about?

Have me back

My heart is tender
  my heart is blue
    my heart means nothing in this world without you

My heart is weak
  my heart could be strong
    my heart should be with you
      in a place where we should belong

So tender   so blue
  how do I live in this world without you

I give these words to have you back
  listen to me for my words are facts

You came into my life
  and reenergized love
    and gave my heart
      new strength from above

I long so hard to have you near
  take my heart back I need you even more my dear

Life is short
  but my love for you is long
    I cry at night, just to keep my heart warm

Lovers come and lovers often times may go

Yet with me my love
  you shall never want for more

As for me my love
  I promise to never let you go.

-t.alfonso williams

………….at last one finds love, and a small unexpected misunderstanding throws it into mayhem and we find our heart begging to make things right.

Shadows

In life we all walk a very thin line
  which consists of our life time

Some may walk bold and ever so cold

While some may walk meek
  with wings of love beneath their feet

Life is love and the breath we take
  alone with the choices we make

Some are wrong
  some are right

As we beg the Lord
  to just help us
    to see the light.

-t.alfonso williams

………..as humans we are the only creatures on earth with the ability to select the things that we wish to do in life.

First Kiss

That first kiss is always the best
  others follow, but never as the first

That first kiss from you
    made my head spin
        like that of wild stars out of control

My heart raced as if to say
  I can't stop

You didn't just kiss me
  you really
      truly kissed me

Your lips
  so soft to mine

Your lips and that of your arms around me
  give that warm feeling of love

Not just love
  but that
    I love you feeling of love

The best love, is love given
  and love given in return
    in the same moment
      of time.

-t.alfonso williams

*This was written because I remembered the kiss of a lady that I was falling in love with.
Sometimes it is like that, something as simple as a kiss, her smell and a cool gentle wind.*

Patiently

Your skin so soft
  I love touching you

Lips so sweet
  I taste them each time you speak

Eyes so warm
  I drop to my feet

But I am a man
  yet why oh Lord do I act so weak

You walk into the room and I smell that sweet perfume
  that intoxicates my mind and makes my heart so blind

You walk with grace and make the heads of men
  forget their place each time you enter their space

For I am blessed to have you my dear
  for I am blessed to hold you so near
    for I am blessed to hold the key to your heart
      for I am the one who knew how to wait patience and smart

Yes   oh yes   I took my time
  the only way a true man
    could capture your heart

For only I could see
  that which a woman
    who saw the patients of me waiting for thee.

By the way, thank you Lord

                                        -t.alfonso williams

… … … … … … …*sometimes it pays to have patience and wait.*

May I Speak

I really have something that I must share with you
   it has been on my mind and I must tell you

You caught my eyes when I first saw you
   and I liked everything at the time about you

You were so kind so gentle and above all so sweet

Your conversations were always so understanding
   never a threat nor too demanding

Each time that my eyes looked upon you
   I saw a beauty that was a blessing given by God to you

When we go out to dinner
   oh I love the way that you shine
      in your own way, you let the world know, that you are mine

No matter how bad things are
   you find a way to take away the hard part

No matter what you do in the kitchen for us to eat
   you take your time and make it a special treat

You never argue, you never fuss
   you keep life simple with love and trust

These are the things that I had to say
   I took them from my heart, because I had no other way

I care for you so very much
   because my heart, you will always touch.

-t.alfonso williams

The Robbing of Time

In the quiet, still of the night we lay

The only sound is that of the wind blowing, so gently,
   as it carries the smell of the soft summer rains

The darkness is our cover from eyes that wish to see

We lay in the arms of one another, safe away from harm
   as I race my fingers along the path of your soft gentle body,
     with your sweet smell that intoxicates my senses,
       with pride I hold thee

Never wanting this moment to end,
   for wishing to rob time and steal this moment of peace, forever!

With your head resting on my chest, your hair at my nostrils
   reminding me of an herbal garden of love
     you turn your head to look up at me with eyes opening in one motion
       lips wet and luscious, you press to mine
         ooooh   so soft   gentle and delicious
           my head ever so light, as if to leave my body

Your tongue makes love to mine
   passion we both experience

The blood rushes to our heads
   and makes a turnaround to the tips our feet
     traveling high and hot through our bodies

We hold each other with the lock of passion
   upon soft gentle sheets of Egyptian cotton
     which is our refuge
       of love.

-t.alfonso wiliams

.........*for only true lovers can understand these moments in time,*
   that they wish to steal, forever!

My Likes

Like strawberries are your lips
   so wild   so sweet
      I love to taste them just before you speak

Like a rose you look so good
    yet you require one to be gentle for the touch

Like chocolate
   so soft……..so smooth…….so sweet

Like the sun
   you continue to shine
      which keeps bright thoughts on my mind

Like the clear tropical air
   so fresh with a gentle breeze
     you keep my heart at ease

Those are the likes that I feel for you

So is my heart that keeps me with you.

-t.alfonso williams

… … ……...add to this some flowers, a fine dinner, and she'll fall back in love with you.

Do you Remember Me

I remember the time of yesterday
  when each day was a new day

I remember the time of yesterday
  when each minute had to count

I remember when you would only
  let my eyes see you at your best

I remember when the moment of seeing each other
  we would caress

I remember when it was only you and I

I remember the long nights
  of not wanting to say good-bye

I remember you driving away and making that last turn
  and suddenly you were gone

Now I only remember
  the memories of two loving hearts
    that once were unbreakable
      and who only wanted to be one with the other
        for always
          and a day.

-t.alfonso williams

… … … … …two hearts that lost touch, yet memories still hold on.

Happy Am I

You walk   you turn   you stop

You walk   you smile   you greet me.

I see you   I smile   I greet you

We talk

I listen   you speak

I speak   you listen

You speak   I listen

May I see you tomorrow?

Yes

You say

Happy am I
You walk away
Happy am I
Happy am I
Hope you are happy too
I hope.

-t.alfonso williams

… … … … … … … …Two people meeting for the first time in a marketplace and catching the eye of one another, is this a nice day or what? Time put into slow motion.

Hearts of the Wind

Two mighty vessels, each traveling alone in a misty fog
   not aware of the other, each sailing alone in the dark

This went about for many times you see,
   for hearts of the same never seem to find each other
      we must all agree

One clear day when all was fair
   the sky was clear and sea gulls danced in the air

The two mighty vessels crossed the others path
   and in passing they each said hello, with sails of their great mass

This went on a few more times you see
   then one day, one ship asked, I see you sail this way often times passing me

The two mighty vessels each lowered their sails
   and shared conversations of sometimes dark and lonely tales

Time had passed in their conversations with each,
   they had more in common than just cargo and treats

So one asked the other, why not lower your sail and travel with me,
   we each could save time and our travels could last endlessly

So that they did and today as you see,
   we have all gathered together to celebrate their joyous victory.

              May the sands of time never leave your feet
              as you walk with God and follow his beat.

              -t.alfonso williams

… … …..as the best man for my friend Jerome and his new wife Shirley, my words of celebration.

Love Awaits

Without a knock on the door it comes
    her entrance is at will
Without a warning she surprises
    as a thief in the night
She starts with a small prick
    to the heart
    for it is more vulnerable
Her appetite consists of small bites
    until she has acquired a taste for it
Slowly she weakens her victim by consuming
    the logic of thought
Over time she takes over the strength of her prey
    if only allowed
The strong fight her to gain back control
Her mate is in the heart of the other
    fighting to unite them
Tears of happiness screams with joy from the two hearts
The force of love and her mate links the chain between the two hearts
Love has over powered once more
    two new hearts
    love and her mate
    must now venture
    to discover two more new hearts.

-t.alfonso wiliams

… … … … ….just like the struggle for good and evil to claim a victory in the minds of you and I, so is the battle for love to unite two unforgiving hearts.

Blind Dreams

You set alone and dream of love
    like most young women do

Hoping for the prince of love
    to come and rescue you

For we know that it's not true
    that which men are thought to do
        they hardly ever come to rescue you

For it is up to you my daughter
    to do what you must do
        for it is up to you
            to rescue you.

-t.alfonso williams

… … … … … … … … … … … … … from fathers to our daughters,
don't believe in the dreams of others, but in the dreams of self.

Love Is

If this is love
   then let me love

If love is the sun
   then let me shine

If love is a river
   then let me flow

If love is a mountain
   then let me stand bold

If love is a flower
   then let me grow

-t.alfonso williams

… … … … …why must we bother love, can we jst let it be?

Rain Walker

Cold winds that blow upon ones face

Dancing rain that moves with grace
    can it hide the tears of my face

Love is just a word we use
    for some to impress
        for some to express
            for some to abuse

I walk alone

I cry amongst the rain
    to hide from the world the mystery of my pain

How long do I walk

How long must I cry

How long before the pain in my heart
    of my love
        decides to die.

-t.alfonso williams

………………….*a simple walk in the rain to masquerade pain.*

So Rich I Be

Oh I'm rich, this you cannot see
nor do I have a ton of money
to pay for all that I see

Oh I'm rich, within my heart
that's what makes my decisions
so very smart

Yes I'm rich with love abound
you won't see me walking with a frown

I'm so rich with love that cares
take my hand
oh yes I'll share

I love you
do you love me

Put a smile on your face and see
how contagious the richness
of love can be.

t.alfonso williams

… … … … … … … … …..the richness of love cost nothing, yet it's priceless.

My Secret

In secret I watch you

In secret I love you

In secret I dream of you

But secrets are just dreams that we imagine while awake

Dreams are the shadows of thoughts
   which wonder between reality and fantasy

Yet where am I, when I look at you.

-t.alfonso williams

………………….the mind of a man as he admires a special woman in secret.

Young Heart Old Love

A heart so young that has no shame
   that enjoys life as if it were a game

A heart so new that invites love through
   without stress or pain

A heart that is open for love to do
  just what it wishes to do

Then came Old Love and said, do to me
   that which I have heard of you to do

Sure, come Old Love and try to hurt me
   if you can, for I am a stronger man

For Old Love is smart and it tells the young heart,
   don't try me young man I'll hurt you, I can

The young foolish heart screams and shouts
   never to understand what true love is about

Old Love is wise and waits its time to show
   the young heart of a swift and silent blow

While young heart turns its back and walks away
   thinking to play with Old Love another day

Old Love is smart and plays the young heart
   for a few more days, just to make him think he's hard

Young heart thinks that Old Love has given up
   yet walks away to think that he can play with Old Love any day

Young heart rested one day not knowing that Old Love was near,
   Old Love then shot the young heart, with no fear

Young heart was awakened and started crying
   and for the rest of the day, though he was dying

Old Love told young heart, never mess with me,
   for I make my best move when you sleep.

-t.alfonso Williams

Big Love

I walk in the rain to avoid people from seeing my pain within

Love has, nor does it show mercy on my heart

The pain marinates itself into my bones

I have no feelings
   my mind is empty
      my mouth is numb
         there is no hunger in my stomach for nourishment

I long for sleep to escape my pain for rest
   and for the security from that
      which dominates me.

                                        -t.alfonso Williams

*..........yes it hurts, you can't rub it away, you can't take a pill, you can't get it drunk, it's just there to let you know that **I**, "Love" has tattooed your heart. There is no rest until I decide to let go.*

WARNING: Love is harmful to most hearts. May cause blurred vision & dizziness, lost logic of reality can also occur.

Mirror

Outside of you I stand
    trying so hard to look through the misty window of your heart

Your warmth comforts my soul

Your smile offers hope within my heart

Your touch gives me the willingness to continue

Why, can I not stand outside of myself and see
    that which others see.

-t.alfonso williams

…………why is it so easy for others to see us from the outside.

Ha Love

Ha love, ha love
   and how are you feeling today
      you look so fine
         am I blessed that you are a friend of mine

Ha love, ha love
   as I look at you today
    I ask the Lord a special prayer
    to bless your soul today

Ha love, ha love
   please come here my dear
     so that I may whisper into your ear
      that for none other but you to hear

Ha love, ha love
   again I say, I'm so glad you are mine
    as I look into your soft kind eyes
      to discover that I had truly made the greatest find.

-t.alfonso williams

... ...something sweet to place deep into her ear
*   to show that your love has no fear.*

Holding On

For why...........for what
　For what...........for why

To have and to hold
　to love and to be set free

Freedom is not free until it is free

Yesterday was then and then there is no more

Within yesterday were love, beauty and adventure

For yesterday is now a dark and forgotten past
　unable to conclude its unobtainable conclusions

Yet we often travel its back streets trying to regain something
　which is no longer included into our now

We hope for that second try
　which will satisfy that lost part of the heart
　　that has yet to heal from wounds of joyful memories

So much yesterday
　so little today
　　with no tomorrow.

-t.alfonso williams

............a crystal glass filled with milk has broken, can we get "it" back?

Seasons of Love

Spring arrives and love is in her eyes
        peace is in her heart and happiness is in her stride

She searches for love and it seeks her out
        at last her love now screams and shout

Summer comes with passion and heat
        and all is wonderful and never so sweet

Endless love with nothing to spare
        forbidden fruit for love why should they care

The Autumn leaves bring change in the air
        and forbidden love is not as great as their summer flair

The air of the heart is cool and not as warm
        for the summer heat now burns not from their summers love

Winter comes and she brings with her snow
        she covers her love and loves no more

The cold of her heart is here to stay
        and no longer does she feel it necessary
            to love for another day.

-t.alfonso williams

… … … … … …seasons change and so does love.

Forbidden

Have you ever dreamed a dream at night
   of someone you know
      that really wasn't right

Why did I dream of a person you see
   a person who means little to me

I was awakened in the middle of the night
   with this dream of you and I
      with an abundance of lust that I know not to be right

Why oh why I need to know
   you of all people that I know

Now within when I look at you
   hiding a secret though of you

Time after time I ask myself why,
   why would I have a dream one night
      of you and I doing something that was never to be true in life

Now and then when I look at you
   this secret dream I wish so bad to share with you

But if I had the nerve to share this dream with you,
   you would only turn and slap my face
      a new shade of blue.

-t.alfonso williams

………… not sure if this has ever happened to you or not, but I had this crazy dream about someone who I only speak to from time to time. For the life of me I question my subconscious over and over.

CLUE I

Women enjoy meeting men that they see, with a possibility of having a future.
The question comes up sooner or later in the relationship about a commitment.
Now, women want this spontaneous answer from men, which makes a man's brain
go into overdrive for an answer without turning the woman off.
He then asks himself, do I say what she wants to hear or do I give her an honest
answer which may upset her and she wants no more to do with me.
Ladies, most men are not afraid of the word "commitment", it's that spontaneous
question that you throw at them without a warning that makes them run off.

Answer
You want him to make a commitment with you correct? You really like this guy,
he has it going on, and you see some future in him and that's a good thing.
Now in order to get, you must also be willing to give. What are you bringing to the
table for him to see a reason for him to make a commitment?
Oh, by the way not just your body. Please!!

-Are you special in his life, by making him feel comfortable with you?
-Are you a taker, someone who always looks for something, just because you feel
that you are woman and there is some unwritten rule to say
that he must give to you. Remember, giving works both ways.
-Are your conversations mostly logical, without disrespect of each other?
-Can you carry an open conversation, to disagree without being disagreeable?
-Is their fun and laughter with each of you, for most of the time?

The heart that beats
Hear to the souls which cry
They give a silent voice to the ears that wish to listen

-t.alfonso williams

Chapter II

Is it worth

Lost I was in the forest of sin
    I had no way out
      I was too far in

Shame I brought myself
    and my family too

A love for something, that was never true
    lie, cheat or steal……….. that was my day

To satisfy my love
    I saw it no other way

I would cheat   I would beat any I met
    just so that I, could get my high

Every day I wanted to run away
    but I was hooked
      my soul was booked with the devil

Sometimes I would cry and pray,   oh Lord just let me die today
    my soul was promised for the devil you see
      for no more good was to come of me

The streets were my home both night and day
    when did I sleep I hear you say
      no one knows not even me
        for me to sleep would be a tragedy
          or maybe a relief for the demon in me

You don't understand what I must go through
    just pray for me, and hope that you, never will too

When I die and if you pray
    ask the Lord to show the rest of us
    a better way.

-t.alfonso williams

………………drugs are a selfish habit which has no love for anyone.

What was life like

The head stone reads, 1949 to 1989
    yet I ask, what did he do in between that time?

Was he a man of steel
    with plenty of love and appeal

Was he a man of hate
    which always showed upon his face

Was he a man blessed with God's good grace
    who cared for others as he walked this place

Did he walk the way of man
    not caring that God held his future in his hand

Did he walk in the light of God
    who strongly knew his heart

What is life
    but a breath of air

Here today…………..gone tomorrow
    a little pain……………..a little rain
        a little sunshine……………a little sorrow

Quest what?
    No more tomorrow!!!!

-t.alfonso williams

……………….most headstones read the birth and death,
but what about that of the in between?

What Time Is It

A baby comes into this world with many tiny tears
  we scream and shout with joy
    in hopes for this baby
      to see many happy years

An old man dies
  with no more suffering
    and no more pain
      and fades away in our memories
        for nothing more to gain

Life goes on and so does time
  we ponder to ask
      what in life do we really leave behind

How we live life
  well
    it's up to you

But whatever you do
  do it with something
    that God and life
      will be proud of you.

-t.alfonso williams

… … … … … … … ….*what is life to you and how precious is it for you?*

Did you love today?

Who have you loved today?

Was it the man begging on the street
   who was looking for a handout
      to get something to eat
or was it in your mind, that he just wanted
   to purchase a bottle of wine.
While you walked down the street with new shoes
    on your feet and something sweet
      in your hand as you eat

Who have you loved today?
Are you the man or woman of the hour
   who holds the power, to grant a chance
      for a fellow worker to advance

Who have you loved today?
Do you feel, that all should think and act like you
   with earthly possessions that only makes life easy for you

Do you look down on people with less than thee,
   yet knowing inside your heart,
     that you are weaker than any eyes
       will ever see.

For who have,
   you loved today?

-t. alfonso williams

… … …..just be careful that the feet you step on today, aren't connected to the butt you may have to kiss tomorrow!!

Just move on

I touch the sky and say good-bye
  to all the dreams that never were

I left upon a midnight train
  to start again in a different frame

Many laughed upon my dreams with doubts
  never to understand the value of what life is all about

For they had never lived outside their world
  as I and others had tried to tell
    the truth of a far better world

People that live day by day
  to think that their way was the only way

Sick and tired it came to be
  living amongst people who had no idea
    of true reality

So I made it in my mind
  it's time to go
    and connect with people of a different flow

It's a shame to see
  people who think they know it all to be

Yet, live in a world that is too blind
  and will never be able to see.

-t.alfonso williams

……………………living among the walking dead isn't healthy for the living.

A Secret Ear

For I walk with you
  through the forbidden gates of your past
    and listen with you dark dreams of tales
      that only God and me would ask

You have told me things that I would fear
  as I would listen with my ear
    a tear would sometimes come to me
      from the voice of a heart that is so sweet

In life we sometimes feel that God has abandoned us
  all because we failed to understand and trust

For life is all the things we do and learn
  sometimes we gain reward
    sometimes we are burned

God is always there, yet we know not where
  his Holy Spirit travels where we would not dare

Yes life is hard and lots of times ruff
  yet within your heart
    please find a way
      and never give up God's trust.

-t.alfonso williams

.............*we sometimes listen to the secrets of friends which trust to share,*
      yet we all store some dark past that we keep locked away in yesterday.

My head hurts

Woman if I could
    just get you outta my head I would

For some strange reason
    I can't sleep at night
        get outta my head and let me sleep at night

All I wish to do
    is to sleep all night
        so get outta my head
            and let me sleep tonight

I fell in love with a woman
    who really ain't right for me
        keeping me up all night
            making me dream of things that ain't right for me

Get outta my head
    get outta my head
        woman please just get outta my head

Am I betta off dead
    with you always in my head

Get outta my head
    get outta my head
        woman please I ask get outta my head
        and please will you
            get outta my bed!

-t.alfonso williams

… … … … … … ….now this what you would call a weak brother or one that is whipped !

The Healer

Yes your heart has been broken and much was taken from you,
    but life isn't over and there is still hope for you
He broke your heart but he didn't steal it away,
    you still have life even for another day
A broken heart can be healed, this I prove to be real
A fragile heart needs lots of love and care,
    and treated gentle without despair
Extend your arms and give me your hand,
    let me show you the love of a real man
Tender and kindness is only required of you,
    and I can show you that I can heal your heart back new
Love is so simple but some make it hard,
    because only the foolish can break a woman's heart
A compliment or two, in a day for you, to let you know I think of you
A phone call to say, how are things going for you today
Some flowers to just brighten your day,
    to make you feel happy and special that way
Dinner for two, just me and you,
    with candle lights that glow, so that I may see your love grow
A walk in the park while I hold your hand,
    to let all that see us know, that I am your man
A kiss after dark, a smile from deep within your heart
For I am the healer, never to run you away
    with me my love, you will always wish to stay.

-t.alfonso williams

… … … … …..*one man's lost is another man's gain, so don't give up hope.*

CLUE II

Be careful who you share your secrets with.
Sometimes that person you think is your friend could be your enemy.

You have an argument with your man about something that the two of you cannot seem to agree on. So you take it to this friend who gives you this knowledge of information to ensure you a correct plan of guaranteed comfort. In telling this so called friend you also ask that, they shouldn't share your thoughts with others. Well sorry, she has just gotten an earful of fresh gossip to share with the world and she has told everyone that you are the biggest and weakest fool in town.

I'm sorry dear, but you should learn in life to choose your friends better. Men and women should learn to communicate better to avoid battles. Things like miscommunication and simple misunderstandings can fuel a war in a relationship, and it doesn't have to be. Learn to listen to one another, stop this idea of you gotta be right all the time and learn to agree without being disagreeable. Oh yeah, stop this thing about having to say the last word ladies, "please just shut up". Having the last word means nothing.
It's okay to vent to someone, but approach with caution.

The World in which we live

The following pages are based upon the society that we live in and the social issues we face or sometimes ignore.
Read with an open mind.

Chapter III

Little Brother

All alone you stand
With a made in America, gun in your hand
You scream……..you shout
    no one wishes to understand, the words from your mouth
So strong………so free………..your own self creativity
Smart with undiscovered knowledge of self
    ain't afraid of nothing……….or no one………..just your self
Smart without compare
    yet blind to knowledge of self, without a care
Like a lion you roam and hunt the streets alone
Trying to stay alive………to only survive
Only one enemy…….. which you…………yourself could really defeat
    that one enemy wishes to keep you down
        so that you can never stand and walk like a man on your feet
He loves to put it in the hearts of others, to fear you and make up evil lies about you
For others are blind and cannot see, that they too are the enemy and not just thee
You run through the jungles of the streets, hiding and dodging the other man's dirty beat
No job your heart and mind can never seem to find
Yet, you find a way to avoid unjust arrest and still stay alive
There is so much in your young heart you wish to do
But no one wants to give a second look at you
You run in packs with those who think and look like you,
Only because ain't much else for you and the gang to do
The only way for you to stay alive,
Is to act like them and talk the same street vibe
But some day if you just hang in there,
God will show you, that he really cares
  and all the dreams, you wish within
      will someday come true
        and please, the real man
          locked away in you.

-t.alfonso williams

……………………..*as it is said;* **"a mind is a terrible thing to waste"**.

Statuesque

You buy things you know you don't need
   just to satisfy your fashion greed

You spend big money for this and big money for that, ask yourself,
   is buying this making you acceptable for living like that

Gucci, Prada, and Hilfiger too,
   do you think that they give a care about you

You spend your money and most of your time,
   trying to be accepted by people who don't care for your kind

The money you waste on this junk today
   could be the same money that would bring you from a crunch some day while old and gray

We waste more money than any race, just to be accepted
   to live and smile in some racist's face

Yes we are first in line to purchase a new style
   yet when it comes to education our kids are lost in denial

A flat screen, a diamond ring and maybe a few other unnecessary worldly things
   so when was the last time you introduced your child to something that made their mind sing

A better education and knowledge of self
   will take you further than you have ever felt

Champagne dreams with low budget pockets
   how do you plan to get ahead trying to ride on rockets

Study the Ant, as the Bible says, learn his ways
   to survive and gain respect in the world you live in today.

-t.alfonso williams

............*we as a people waste more money on foolishness and non-sense, trying to be what?*
"Stop playing to play and play to win"

Why am I so angry

Am I mad at my mother
   for bringing me here

Am I mad at my father
   for not caring and holding me near

Am I mad at my sister
   the one that I should love and trust

Am I mad at my brother
   who has made it in the world
      and making many times as much

Am I mad at others for my deeds
   that even I can't explain
      yet I continue not to succeed

For whom should I blame, other than me
   for this unruly mass
      that even God will not bless

Dropping out of school was the thing for me
   in my mind I saw a lot more possibilities

Who do I love
   who do I trust
      in the streets making money or jacking someone up

Life these days don't matter to me
   all I want to do is make money and act as if I'm free

It won't be long before my days will be gone
      and all I'll leave behind
         is for someone to sing
            a sad, sad song.

-t.alfonso Williams

… … … … … …the seeds of our future that no one bothers to nourish

Brains in the butt

Shame you have no sense I see,
   not for woman, man, or me
You walk the streets like a clown,
   thinking its hip with your pants hanging down
No one really wishes to be bothered by you,
   you show the world it has no respect for you
Trying to prove something you wish only to be,
   just a lost child with no dignity
You run with those who are your same,
   but the world calls you by a different name
Your brains I see must be in your butt,
   cause that's the way you have for us to look
You have no respect for yourself I see,
   still a follower of a misunderstood breed
Ask to explain why you dress this way,
   even you don't know why, nor can you explain
Mothers and fathers have died for you,
   to give you a world of a different view
They died for respect and dignity,
   so that you could live in a world, someday to be free
So pull up your pants and expose your mind,
   to a world that you need not to hide
The mind you have should be exposed,
   to a symphony of thoughts your heart could compose
So much is in this world for you,
   the dignity and respect is left up to you
Respect is something that is earned by me,
   not forced by one's insecurity
Dignity is how you carry yourself,
   from within how your heart is felt.

-t. alfonso williams

The Walls of Wall Street

I walk the streets for many years
   on which I carried so many tears

My eyes have seen so many of a good man's fears
   with the pain and suffering of many years

Good men die and bad men lie
   while women and children stand alone and cry

Heartless men which feast on greed
   just to satisfy their own financial needs

Laws are written and rules are made
   yet some men find it all to be a financial game

You earn today while others lose
   and lie about the financial news

Thieves and thugs you clam not to be
   riding around pimping the world for all to see

Shame on you shame on me
   for letting you get away for free

Someday soon and very soon
   the walls of laws will crumble down on you
      only to meet your doom

And you'll ask the world to have pity for thee
   but never did you have pity on me

Than you and yours will have hell to pay
   for believing that time would let you
      just invisibly slip away.

-t.alfonso williams

............legal loan sharks, pharmaceutical drug dealers and white collar criminals

Shoes of Cinderella

Snake tongue preachers alone with political pimps
    they are but a few who head the list of liars
        that stand in front of me and you

They give up their day jobs for power and might
    lying for our votes and swearing they'll make things right

Many have little money to start, yet they find plenty to burn
    as they come across my flat screen spreading their words and germs

Divide and conquer is the name of the true game
    this is how they make a reputation for their name

Let me show you facts, I'll air it on radio and TV
    knowing you can't prove the research dug up by me

Welfare, socialist, terrorist, militants and civil rights too,
    only to name a few, names that are given to strike fear in you

They'll always inform you on how bad things are
    while lying and screaming, and stashing rotten monies somewhere afar

Looking for dirt in a good persons name
    let's look in their closet, now, we can really shame the blame

Dirty is he which sets by the door
    collecting garbage just to keep a better score

For years they have lied to us
    and told us things about others, who we were not to trust

To control a man's thinking is a great defeat
    and to take away his knowledge, you have just made him weak

A lot of things are placed in front of us not to be true,
    but without knowledge and understanding
        who do you really trust

Spending and spending money as it falls freely from the air
    providing and protecting for the rich

who really don't give a care

Poor people hustling money with barely enough to meet their needs
    trying to get by, with little hungry mouths to feed
        while some rich fool is being wasteful with greed

A celebrity was said to have murdered, two people some years ago
    why does the media keep it fresh, do you ever stop to ask, or do you know

A little child was kidnapped and murdered, some time ago
    not much was made of it, because the media didn't think so

White collar thieves and corporate thugs which live among us
    begging for our votes and asking us to trust
        while robbing us blind and stealing right in front of us

Right on for America, in God we say that we trust
    so where is the trust in the God that we trust,
        for there is no trust in God,
            because in America
                we only worship the "**Buck**".

                                                -t.alfonso williams

                        ……………….*who wears shoes of Cinderella?*

Preachers of Paradise

Cathedrals in the ghetto I call them to be,
   which takes up blocks amongst the poor and poverty

They stand in vain with no regards of how they stain,
   which brings to shame in Jesus name

I watch them rise in many shapes and size,
   to satisfy the preacher's eyes

On Sunday mornings he begs for more, to pay for dreams he has in store

While outside the Cathedral doors a family starves just asking for a little more

The preacher sees them and tells them to come inside,
   while giving them that same old line, give it to Jesus and he will provide

Father mother and children later walk away, with their heads down and nothing to say,
   old preacher smiles and laughs out loud, I'll see ya'll again, as he is so proud

Old Sister Jones smiles, and shakes the preacher's hand,
   while slipping him the last of her monthly cash

He has no love for none of their salvation, only to satisfy his own greedy temptations

He gets into his car with his first lady too,
   they drive across town pass ghetto streets no longer in view,
      their conversation is long and sweet, trying to decide some expensive place to eat

After dinner they scream and shout praising the lord inside their big old gated house

If thinking members could only see, the phony preachers and what they mean

Their heaven on earth is here today, and the gates of heaven is no place to play

It's ok for one to live well, but playing with God and heaven will grant you a trip to hell

If you are a preacher you need to check your life, by making sure you are living right.

-t. alfonso williams

………………*not all preachers are this bad, just a few shepherds that feed from the flock.*

CLUE III

So the two of you argue too much?
Have you ever stopped to ask yourself why and what you are arguing about.
And now you feel that because of that, the two of you aren't compatible.

Well is arguing good for a relationship?
Some would say no, while others would say its okay or how do you argue?
Are you loud and disrespectful towards one another and out to hurt one another?
Do you bring old garage from the pass to score points while arguing?

Well arguing is something everyone does when we cannot reach an agreement.
Is it bad? It doesn't have to be as long as we stick to the subject. One thing it does
is it gets whatever it is off our chest, while showing concern and showing honesty.
Everyone has an opinion about an issue and its okay to express that opinion with
your mate. Keep in mind that an opinion is a personal expression of feelings. When
two people can express their opinions about something without getting physical or
violent with one another it shows respect and maturity.
In an argument it also helps us to learn one another, our likes and dislikes. An
argument doesn't mean the end of the world or the relationship.
One thing to bear in mind is, "choose your battles".

Memories

These are the memories which also carry tears.
To face and understand our hurt is part of the healing.

-t.alfonso williams

Chapter IV

Real Men Do Cry

Oh yes a man will cry...............not just to offer his final good bye

Oh yes, the world heard me cry
    the day I came into this world and the doctor spanked my behind
        and a tiny tear fell from my father's eye

O yes a man can cry
    the day when I got my narrow butt beat
        for making up a lie and stealing a treat from the store across the street

Oh yes I saw my father cry too
    when they buried his father from Cancer
        and he had to say his final good bye too

Oh yes I've seen a many tears fall from a grown man's eye
    when Dr. King's life was taken, a man who won a Pulitzer Prize
        everyone's heart was taken and so was a good life mistaken

I saw a man who badly wanted to raise and feed his family too
    but another man wouldn't allow that of him to do
        because he felt he was privileged to

Some years ago, I saw a good man who had to bury his first son
    who was gunned down by some thugs
        that ran and played, and did it all in the name of fun

So sad   so sad
    oh yes to see, a grown man cry tears of sympathy,
        sometimes they are invisible, not to be seen by you or me

Oh yes a man will cry
    to watch his little girl marry and move away
        in hopes for her to come back some day

I saw a man who could never cry
    when he came home to tell his family
        that his job had closed the doors, and told all employees good bye

I saw an old man who had to continue to work
    so that he could feed his family
        and take orders from a young and foolish jerk

I felt the tears which had fallen from my own eyes
when a woman I loved broke my heart and left me to cry

Yes a man can cry...........by all means, real men do cry
never let someone tell you a different kind of lie

And yes I too had to cry, when I saw my own father die
from the pain and suffering that took my grandfather's life

You see a real man will do, that which he has to do
to keep his woman safe, his children feed
and making sure, all are comfortable, when they go to bed

He will sometimes sit alone in the late hours of the night
thinking and crying, when all are out of sight,
praying to the Lord to keep
warmth, shelter and food for his family to eat

Oh yes, a real man will cry too
so never let no one take that hope
away from you.

-t.alfonso Williams

............remember this, God made us all to be able to "Love and Cry", even Jesus cried!

After Your Love Has Gone

 In life love comes into one's heart with the hope of lasting forever, but the truth of the matter is, love is only a temporary thing, a feeling that intoxicates the heart.

 It departs our presence by death,   by separation in a marriage   or a relationship that we were so sure of.

 However the departure is, it hurts. No matter who you are, no matter how strong. The one left standing on the side of the road as love makes its journey into the sunset with that part of our heart that kept us whole, carries the biggest hurt.

 The only thing that it leaves, are the shadows of our yesterdays that are known to our senses, as memories.

 Memories that we store in a dark room in the back of our hearts, as we hold the only key, to its entrance.

 And so occasionally we walk down its dark halls, just to unlock the door for a brief fix, hoping to leave, some of our hurt, inside.

-t.alfonso williams

 I was inspired to write this for an old girlfriend from back in the day, who had later married. I was back in Memphis in 2000 and ran into her, she explained to me about her marriage and the death of her husband plus the hurt from her loss.

Take away nine

Here I lay cold in a hole from a nine
   that stole my soul
You get to walk away for free away from me
   little sisters we thought to be
      sharing love and with spirits free
Late nights, talking on the phone about dreams
   of tomorrow now dead and gone
My mother, your mother were like sisters too
   why would you take my breath from me
We shared love........we shared time
   I would sometimes give you my very last dime
Did I give too much or not enough
  did you have to take my life
    just to make it all up
Yes I now rest in my peace
  but how are your thoughts affecting thee
Oh yes it's cold down here
   without my mother's heart to hold me near
    but the good thing about
       I have no fear
You stole my life
  you stole my time
    now it's over are you happy inside
Can you sleep at night
  do you rest in the day
Oh yes, I'm still with you
  in your mind
    forever and a day.

-t. alfonso williams

This was a poem I wrote and dedicated to a dear friend whose daughter was murdered by a so called friend in the summer of July 2003 in Memphis.

Another Innocent Demonized Sister

A shining star for all to see
    was the dream for you to be
Young and pretty with a lot of sense
    your time was precious and very well spent.
You had the world in front of you
    and dreams to do what you wanted to
Cautious you were day by day
    cause your parents protected you in many ways
Smart you were in books with ease
    when it came to men, you had weak knees
One day a pretty boy came along
    with lie after lie, he led you on
Your mind was saying, he is no good for me
    but your heart kept saying, do as you want, it's free
He told you lies and gave you dreams
    just to see if you would follow the stream
Then one day he said to you
    I love you baby, do you love me too!
You were raised about the sins of men
    and all the troubles, they would get you in
So he took you home without a fight
    while trying to make love with you, most of the night
He served you wine, he served you weed
    to put your strong mind at ease
You grew tired and weak
    then decided to give in
        then asked yourself is this a sin?
Before letting him enter you,
    you ask if he were wearing a protection too?
Baby please, put your mind at ease
    for it is only you
        that I've ever had
            for this is true
                he sweetly tells you
If this is true for you
    then this is my first time too!
The next morning when she had awakened
    she looked and asked, am I mistaken
She looked beside her and there he was
    with a look of happy that he had scored

Baby, baby do you still love me
we made love without protection
I'm afraid don't you see
Oh baby, oh baby what are you shouting for
I made love with you this I never done before
Now many weeks have passed
and the boy you met
you saw the last
The doctor's visit you made last week
he has something to tell you
that ain't too sweet
You have a demon living inside of you
you find it not to be a baby too
oh you wish, that was true
The doctor tells you,
you don't have long for life on earth
so do what you can, to make it worth
You sit in his office, quiet as a mouse
watching your life flash
with silent tears on his couch
Then you get up, lost and walk away
do I take my life
or do I
fight this plague?
You tell yourself, there is still hope for me
I'll fight this thing that's trying to take me
You changed your life style and the way you eat too,
you are now doing things you though that you would never do
Now you spend your days and weeks
telling others about what they can do
to fight this nightmare dream
which came true to you
Brothers, sisters
Black, brown, white, and yellow too
there is something that we all can do.
Just because you aren't infected
none the less
you can't reject it!
Don't you know if most of the AIDS women were white,
America would be in front of this fight!
Put pressure on the government and politicians too
about this thing that is destroying most families
not just me, but you too!

One thing that I must leave for you to do
        is please be careful of what you put your body through
                don't let someone deceive you
                for a moment of evil
                        that will disease you
Life is precious and sweet for you,
        never let the wrong person take advantage of you.

                                    -t.alfonso williams

………….just a simple story of the wolf in sheep's clothing taking advantage of the weak and a small word with great damage to the human body. AIDS has no friends and it crosses every race, culture and community without shame.

Dark Fruit

Love and life are given from God above
  the seed of the spirit which house the soul

All God's children are his precious gifts
  and no man has the right to take that away

Hands reach out to show no harm

Eyes are there yet which not to see

Another dark fruit robbed from our tree
  taken with no remorse or sympathy

A mother's tears floods our streets
  another heart has broken in repeat

The hands of the guilty have again been set free
  to celebrate another unjust victory

America has never protected her dark fruit in need
  she turns her back to pretend not to see

Where the victim becomes the villain
  and the blind has eyes yet refuse to see

Dark fruit to America which no longer has taste
  she searches for another to shame and disgrace

Dark fruit once so loyal and so sweet
  now has thieves which cut at our feet

Dark fruit our mothers will continue to bear
  we will still love our fruit
    even if America doesn't give a care.

-t.alfonso williams

………….to remember and learn how unjustly our brothers and sons have died.

Hate of Fear

For one to show hate without reason
   interpreters that of fear within

While ignorance contaminates the heart

Preconceived prejudice which obstacles
   misdirect the true value of one

An obligation to be accepted by fools
   which gather with internal practice to make the rules

An evil which lives in the heart
   blinded by fear and set apart

Control for your own protection
      to run from fear, afraid that someday,
         the pain that you gave away
            will come back and hunt you
               in the same miserable way

A man creates the evil for that he lives
   yet only birth and death are equal in all that men fear.

-t.alfonso williams

… ….for a man to hate another for no reason, shows himself to be foolish.

CLUE IV

There are no good men left in the world
Well I guess you are right, if you think like that and listen to the wrong people.

There are more good men around than you think. Let me ask you this, are you a good woman? You see a good woman knows what she wants and she doesn't jump on the first train leaving the tracks just to say that she's got a man. She knows how to carry herself to attract the right man. Sure she'll get a few bad bites and she'll throw them back into the water, but chances are she will get a good one.
She sometimes consults with a friend or two for advise, but she keeps it to a minimum making sure that only a little information about her and her man are offered.
She doesn't blame every man for the wrongs of one man's past acts, if she does, she will never find a good man, too busy blaming.
A good man loves a strong woman with a taste of honey to balance her heart.
She also has a good spirit that glows in the presents of others which shows confidence in her personality.
She's a good listener and a good communicator, when it comes to her and her man if there is a problem within their relationship, she can balance the feelings.
She has forgiveness within her heart, if she knows that it will bond their relationship.
She knows that what it took to get him is the same thing it takes to keep him.
These are but a drop in the bucket of pointers, that a good man looks for, in a good woman.

Made in the USA
Columbia, SC
20 June 2022

61911041R00039